# A Soldier's Heart,
# A Shepherd's Calling

*30 Day Devotional for Leaders*

*Stories, of Sacrifice, Strength, and Shepherding from the Front Lines of War and Ministry.*

## JD Drinkard

ISBN: 979-8-9941057-2-6

Printed in the United States of America
First edition

*Endure hardship with us like a good soldier of Christ Jesus. – 2 Timothy 2:3*

## Table of Contents

# Foreword

There's a reason the soldier and shepherd metaphors are so prevalent in Scripture. They both involve sacrifice. They both demand vigilance. And they both require a heart ready to bleed for those under your care.

I've lived as both.

From the deserts of Iraq to orphanages in Eastern Europe... from the battlefield to the mission field... from the frontlines of war to the quiet moments in my children's bedrooms, praying over them after a long trip away... I've been shaped by fire and refined by grace.

This devotional isn't written from a stage. It's written from the dirt. From the roof of a building surrounded by enemy flares. From the third floor of a shelter in Poland that I had to crawl to reach in my wheelchair, just to sit with Ukrainian orphans. From moments where I failed my family by putting the mission first and was shown mercy by a son who still called me 'World's Greatest Dad.'

If you're reading this, I believe God is stirring something in you. Maybe you're a leader. Maybe you're just trying to keep your faith afloat. Maybe, like me, you've found yourself leading from a wheelchair, or from some other place of visible or invisible brokenness.

This 30-day journey is an invitation: to rise when it's easier to retreat, to kneel when pride says stand tall, and to serve when your strength is gone.

Let's lead from the dirt, together.

With gratitude,

JD Drinkard

# Day 1: The Mission Before You

*"Endure hardship with us like a good soldier of Christ Jesus." — 2 Timothy 2:3*

### Called to a Battlefield, Not a Vacation

When I served in the Army, we didn't always get to see the full mission plan. We'd roll out before dawn, adrenaline pumping, radios crackling, unsure of what the day might bring. But we trusted the Commander and moved out anyway. That kind of faith wasn't rooted in full clarity; it was rooted in obedience.

That mindset carried over after I came home. I didn't return in a wheelchair right away, in fact, at first, I looked fine. But I was carrying invisible wounds: a traumatic brain injury and post-traumatic stress that left me disoriented, confused, and angry. I was still a soldier, but I didn't know what battle I was fighting anymore.

That's when I started to see that the Christian life is a lot like combat. You don't get the whole plan upfront. You get the next step, and the command to endure. You might not feel ready. You might feel broken. But that doesn't disqualify you. The mission is still a go.

The call to follow Jesus is a call to endure hardship like a soldier. It's not just about showing up on Sundays, it's about suiting up daily, knowing the enemy is real, but so is your Commander. And He's already overcome.

So, here's what I want you to know: if you feel tired, unqualified, or unsure, that's not a sign to retreat, it's a sign to stay the course. To endure. Because this fight is worth it.

**Prayer:**

Lord, I don't always understand the battle I'm in, but I trust that You've called me for a purpose. Give me strength to endure, courage to follow, and faith to obey even when the road is unclear. Make me a faithful soldier in Your Kingdom, not just in words, but in action. Amen.

# Day 2: Broken, But Not Done

*"But he said to me, 'My grace is sufficient for you, for my power is made perfect in weakness."*
*-2 Corinthians 12:9*

### Leading From the Front — Even When You're Wounded

The blast changed everything. It didn't take my life, but it took pieces of it — physically, emotionally, spiritually. For a while, I thought that meant my mission was over. I imagined that leadership, influence, and service were things I had to leave behind on the battlefield.

Eventually, I found myself in a wheelchair. That was the moment I really wrestled with identity. I wasn't "wounded" in the way people usually think. I had walked off the plane. But the real damage was internal, brain trauma, post-traumatic stress, and a creeping sense of worthlessness. I thought, "What good is a broken soldier?"

But God doesn't lead like we do. He doesn't discard the wounded. In fact, He often calls us to lead from our brokenness, not in spite of it. The world teaches us that strength equals power. But Christ turns that idea upside down. In His economy, grace flows through the cracks.

When I began to let others see the scars, not just the physical ones, but the ones that don't show up on X-rays, that's when real ministry began. People don't need a perfect leader; they need a faithful one. They need someone who's walked through fire and still says, "Follow me as I follow Christ."

So, if you're broken, good. That means there's space for grace. It means you're usable. It means you can lead, maybe more authentically than ever before.

**Prayer:**

Jesus, I offer You my wounds, the ones I try to hide and the ones I'm still healing from. Remind me that I don't have to be whole to be used. I just have to be willing. Use my scars as stories of Your faithfulness. Let others see Your strength in my weakness. Amen.

# Day 3: Strength in Surrender

*"Be strong and courageous." - Deuteronomy 31:6*

## Courage Isn't the Absence of Fear, It's Obedience in the Face of It

People see the uniform, the medals, the wheelchair, and they think I must be strong. But the truth? Most of my strength didn't come from combat training or physical conditioning. It came from moments of desperation, moments when I had nothing left but God.

I remember sitting in the hospital, unsure if I would walk again, unsure if I even wanted to. I wasn't afraid of pain; I was afraid of living a small life. Afraid of becoming invisible. Afraid of being forgotten. That fear was real. But in the middle of it, I heard a whisper in my spirit: *"Be strong and courageous... I will never leave you."*

That's when I began to understand, strength isn't gritting your teeth and pushing through. Real strength comes when you surrender your fear, your pride, and your plans to the

One who goes before you. The courage God calls us to isn't about dominating the battlefield; it's about trusting the Commander when the fog sets in.

Maybe you're in a fog right now. Maybe you feel the weight of the unknown, the pressure to perform, or the fear of failing. But listen, God isn't asking you to be fearless. He's asking you to be faithful.

Courage is saying yes when everything in you says hide. It's leading your family through uncertainty. It's showing up when you feel like quitting. That kind of strength doesn't come from you. It comes from Him.

**Prayer:**

Father, give me the kind of strength that doesn't rely on my own power. Teach me to surrender, not in defeat, but in trust. Let my courage be rooted in Your presence, not my performance. When I am afraid, remind me You are near. Amen.

# Day 4: The Weight of the Pack

*"Carry each other's burdens, and in this way, you will fulfill the law of Christ." - Galatians 6:2*

**You're Not Meant to March Alone**

In combat, no one carries their rucksack solo for long. We help each other redistribute weight, check on each other's footing, keep each other from falling behind. It's a code, an unspoken rule: *You don't leave a soldier behind.*

But in life, especially spiritual life, too many of us try to carry everything ourselves. We think if we're struggling, it's a sign of weakness. So, we hide our burdens behind smiles, polite words, or silence. I've done it. I've led teams, churches, even my own family, while secretly suffocating under the weight of grief, shame, or exhaustion.

For me, one of those burdens was learning how to ask for help. After my injuries, I needed help with the most basic tasks. I hated it. I felt useless. But over time, I started to see something beautiful: when I let others carry part of the load, I was fulfilling a deeper calling, not to be self-sufficient, but to be interdependent.

That's what Christ calls us to. He doesn't just want us to believe; He wants us to belong. To lean on one another. To carry each other's pain, listen without judgment, pray without pretense, and love without conditions.

If you're carrying too much today, this is your permission to set it down. To speak up. To trust someone with your truth. And if you're walking light right now, look around. Someone near you is under a heavy load. Don't let them march alone.

**Prayer:**

Lord, teach me to carry and be carried. Help me to lay down pride and pick up compassion. Make me the kind of brother or sister who lightens the load. And when I'm weary, remind me it's okay to reach out. I wasn't made to walk this road alone. Amen.

# Day 5: Orders in the Dark

*"Your word is a lamp to my feet and a light to my path." - Psalm 119:105*

## Faith Means Moving Even When You Can't See the Whole Map

We used to run night missions under blackout conditions, no headlights, no flashlights, just a dim red glow from our gear. We moved forward slowly, deliberately, often with nothing but a compass, a radio, and the trust that our orders were right. Faith feels a lot like that sometimes.

When I left active duty and transitioned to a life I didn't plan, one that included a wheelchair, chronic pain, and invisible wounds, I felt like I was navigating in the dark. I asked God, "What now?" more times than I can count. I wanted clear answers, bright lights, a roadmap. But that's not how He worked.

What I got instead was just enough light for the next step. A conversation that reminded me I still had a voice. A moment in prayer that pulled me out of despair. An opportunity to serve when I felt forgotten.

God didn't lay out the whole mission plan, but He gave me a lamp. And I've learned that a lamp is enough. A lamp doesn't light the whole valley; it lights the next step. You don't need to see the end to obey the command. You just need to move.

So, if you're waiting on clarity, maybe it's time to stop asking for the whole picture and start trusting the One holding the light. His Word is your lamp. His Spirit is your guide. And your mission isn't behind you; it's right in front of you.

**Prayer:**

God, I want to trust You in the dark. When I can't see the future, give me the courage to take the next step anyway. Light my path one moment at a time and remind me that You go with me, even when the way feels unclear. My trust is in You. Amen.

# Day 6: The Shepherd's Heart

*"I am the good shepherd. The good shepherd lays down his life for the sheep." - John 10:11*

**Lead Like a Shepherd, Not a General**

When I first stepped into leadership roles, I led like a soldier, focused on objectives, outcomes, and discipline. That approach worked in combat, but when I started working with orphans in Ukraine, churches in Uganda, and house parents in Moldova, I realized leadership needed something deeper: a shepherd's heart.

Jesus isn't just our Commander; He is our Shepherd. He leads with sacrifice, not ego. He knows His sheep by name, not by rank. He lays down His life, not just to win a battle, but to redeem the broken. That wrecked me in the best way.

I used to think being a good leader meant staying strong, always having the answer, charging ahead. But God started to show me that real leadership is presence. It's walking slowly through the crowd. It's listening. It's protecting the vulnerable. It's weeping with those who weep.

Whether you're leading a church, a family, a business, or just trying to show up for your friends, remember, you're not called to be a dictator. You're called to be a shepherd. And sometimes that means laying down your rights, your comfort, even your pride, so others can find safety and hope. The world needs fewer generals and more shepherds.

**Prayer:**

Jesus, thank You for being the kind of leader who lays down His life. Teach me to lead with Your heart, to care more about people than positions, more about service than spotlight. Make me a shepherd, not just a soldier. Help me to love well and lead faithfully. Amen.

# Day 7: When the Fight Follows You Home

*"The Lord is close to the brokenhearted and saves those who are crushed in spirit." - Psalm 34:18*

## You're Still in the Fight — But You're Not Fighting Alone

I thought the battle would end when I left the war zone. But I quickly realized the fight had followed me home, in ways I never expected. Some nights I couldn't sleep. Other days I didn't want to get out of bed. I'd snap at my wife, drift from my kids, and find myself staring out the window wondering if I was even still the man I used to be. I didn't understand what was happening to me. The uniform was off, but the war was still raging in my mind.

That's when I started to understand that some battles aren't external. They're spiritual. Emotional. Invisible. Maybe your war zone doesn't involve IEDs or insurgents, maybe it looks like divorce, depression, loss, addiction, anxiety, or shame. But make no mistake: it's a battlefield. And the enemy would love for you to believe that you're alone in it. But you're not.

God isn't just present on the mountaintops, He's *close* to the brokenhearted. He doesn't shame the wounded, He saves them. He doesn't wait for you to get it together; He steps into your mess, your confusion, your weakness.

You may still be in the fight. But now you're not fighting for victory, you're fighting *from* it. Because Christ has already won.

So, take heart, soldier. Keep going, shepherd. This war has already been decided, and you are not alone.

**Prayer:**

Father, I confess that some days the battle feels too heavy. I feel broken, tired, and unsure of my next move. But I believe You are close, even in this. Be my shelter, my strength, and my healer. Remind me that this fight is not mine to win alone. You've already overcome. Amen.

# Day 8: Fire Team Faith

*"Though one may be overpowered, two can defend themselves. A cord of three strands is not quickly broken." - Ecclesiastes 4:12*

**You Weren't Meant to Fight Alone**

In the military, the smallest combat unit is the fire team, usually 3 to 5 soldiers trained to move, fight, and survive together. You live with them, train with them, depend on them. When the bullets start flying, they're the ones you trust with your life.

It's no different in the Kingdom of God.

Too many believers try to go it alone. We act like faith is a solo mission, pray by ourselves, fight temptation by ourselves, fall apart by ourselves. But Scripture is clear: we are stronger *together*. Isolation is where the enemy gains ground.

After the blast and during my recovery, I went through a season where I pulled away from people. I didn't want to be a burden. I didn't want to explain the pain. But isolation nearly took me out. It was only when I opened up to a few trusted brothers, my spiritual fire team, that I started to find strength again.

You need people in your life who will check your six, speak truth when you're drifting, and lift you when you're too weak to move. Not just acquaintances, but warriors who will go to battle with you in prayer, in accountability, and in friendship.

If you don't have a fire team, start building one. If you do, lean on them and be that for them too.

**Prayer:**

God, thank You for not calling me to walk this journey alone. Help me find and build a circle of believers who can fight with me and for me. Make me a faithful brother or sister to those in my fire team. Strengthen our bond and protect us as we stand together for You. Amen.

# Day 9: Marching Orders

*"Therefore, go and make disciples of all nations, baptizing them in the name of the Father and of the Son and of the Holy Spirit." –*
*Matthew 28:19*

**You're Not Waiting for a Mission, You're Already on One**

Every soldier knows what it means to receive orders. You don't argue, stall, or wait for a better time. You *go*. You execute the mission. That mindset doesn't end when the uniform comes off, at least it shouldn't.

Jesus gave us a clear mission: *Go and make disciples.*

It's not optional. It's not just for pastors or missionaries. It's not something you start once your life is cleaned up or your schedule is open. The Great Commission isn't a future assignment; it's your present calling.

But I'll be honest, there were seasons where I treated it like a someday suggestion. I thought, *When I get through this next round of physical therapy… when I'm not in pain… when I feel more qualified...* But God didn't wait for me to be ready. He simply reminded me, *I was still breathing, which means I was still sent.*

That shift changed everything. Whether I was speaking in front of political leaders, pushing my wheelchair through the mud at an orphan camp, or praying with a teammate in a hotel parking lot, it all became sacred ground. Every place was a mission field.

You don't need to wait for new marching orders. You've already got them. The only question is: will you move?

**Prayer:**

Jesus, thank You for trusting me with Your mission. Forgive me for the times I've delayed or doubted my role in it. Open my eyes to see the people You've placed around me. Give me the boldness to speak, serve, and lead with purpose, wherever You've placed me. Amen.

# Day 10: When You Don't Feel Like a Warrior

*"But the Lord said to Gideon, 'Peace! Do not be afraid. You are not going to die.'" - Judges 6:23*

## God Doesn't Call the Brave, He Makes the Called Brave

I've lost count of how many times I've looked in the mirror and thought, *I don't feel like a warrior today.* Sometimes I feel more like Gideon hiding in the winepress than David running toward Goliath. We all do.

Gideon was threshing wheat in secret when God showed up and called him a *mighty warrior.* That had to sound like a joke. Gideon even pushed back: *"How can I save Israel? My clan is the weakest, and I'm the least in my family."* But God wasn't speaking to who Gideon saw; He was speaking to who He created him to be.

I get that now. There were years when I felt completely disqualified, broken by trauma, unsure of my voice, dragging my wheelchair into rooms where I thought I didn't belong. But God kept calling me *warrior*, not because

I felt like one, but because He was making me into one.

You might not feel like a warrior right now. You might feel overlooked, exhausted, unqualified. But God sees something in you that you may not see in yourself. His call isn't based on how strong you feel; it's based on His presence and promise. He's not asking you to be fearless. He's asking you to say yes.

**Prayer:**

God, thank You for seeing something in me I can't always see. When I feel weak or afraid, remind me that You are with me, and that's enough. Make me brave in obedience, even when I feel small. Shape me into the warrior You've called me to be. Amen.

# Day 11: The Silence Between Battles

*"The Lord will fight for you; you need only to be still." - Exodus 14:14*

**Rest Is Not Retreat, It's Readiness**

Between deployments, there's this strange stillness. No firefights, no night ops, no immediate chaos, just waiting. Training. Watching. At first, it feels like a break. But after a while, it can feel like something worse: like you've been forgotten.

I've felt that same silence in my spiritual life. After a season of intense service or suffering, everything just... goes quiet. The adrenaline fades. The momentum stops. And I start asking, *"What now?"* Or worse, *"Did I mess up? Has God moved on without me?"*

But here's what I've learned: silence isn't absence. And rest isn't retreat.

Sometimes God *removes* us from the front lines to *restore* us. He teaches us in the quiet what we couldn't hear in the noise. It's in those still moments, in the recovery room, in the slow hospital days, in the quiet drives between camps, that I've heard Him most clearly.

I used to think that resting meant I was weak. That slowing down meant I'd lost my edge. But Scripture reminds me that the Lord fights for us, and sometimes the bravest thing we can do is *be still*.

So, if you're in a season of quiet, don't rush it. Don't fill it with noise. Let God meet you in it. The silence isn't the end of the story; it's preparation for what's next.

**Prayer:**

Father, when things go quiet, help me not to panic. Remind me that You are still at work, even when I can't see it. Teach me to rest in You, to listen more than I speak, and to be still when You say be still. Prepare my heart in the silence for the battles ahead. Amen.

# Day 12: Scars and Stories

*"They triumphed over him by the blood of the Lamb and by the word of their testimony." - Revelation 12:11*

### Your Wounds Can Speak Life

There was a time when I didn't want anyone to know what I had been through. I didn't want to talk about the blast, the pain, the night terrors, or the anger that sometimes took over when I didn't understand why I had survived. I was ashamed of the struggle; afraid it would make me look weak.

But one day, I spoke at a camp for orphans, kids who had been abandoned, abused, or forgotten. I shared about the things I had seen and the wounds I carried. When I finished, a young boy walked up and said, "I didn't know someone like you could feel like me." That's when it hit me: my scars weren't just reminders of pain. They were open doors for ministry.

In the military, scars are part of the uniform. You carry them. You remember where you got them. They become a testimony of survival. In the Kingdom of God, they're even more; they're a testimony of redemption. When we testify to what God has brought us through, we take ground back from the enemy.

Your scars tell a story, and someone needs to hear it. Don't hide the pain that God has healed. Don't silence the testimony that could set someone else free.

You don't have to wait until you're completely "better." Just be honest. Be available. And trust that your story, told in grace, can change someone's eternity.

**Prayer:**

Jesus, thank You for healing wounds I thought would never stop bleeding. Help me to stop hiding what You've already redeemed. Give me boldness to share my story, not to glorify the pain, but to point to the Healer. Use my scars to speak life and hope to others. Amen.

# Day 13: Leading Through the Fog

*"Trust in the Lord with all your heart and lean not on your own understanding; in all your ways submit to him, and he will make your paths straight." — Proverbs 3:5–6*

## You Don't Need Full Clarity to Lead with Full Surrender

We used to run missions in what we called "zero visibility", dust storms, smoke, blackout conditions. You couldn't see five feet ahead. But we still had to move. Still had to lead. Still had to trust the voice on the radio or the compass in our hand.

Leadership in the fog is hard. Whether you're leading a platoon, a family, a church, or even just trying to lead yourself, there are going to be days when you can't see the next move. You'll question if you're getting it right. You'll doubt your own instincts. And if you're like me, you'll be tempted to take control instead of surrender.

But control is a liar. It promises peace but delivers pressure.

There were times in my life, especially after injury and transition, when I didn't know what the next step looked like. I didn't know if I could provide for my family. I didn't know if I could serve from a wheelchair. I didn't know if my voice still mattered. The fog was thick. But God was faithful.

Proverbs 3 doesn't say "figure it out." It says, "trust in the Lord." That's the command. The promise is that *He* will make the path straight, not easy, not always clear, but straight. On His terms. In His time.

If you're in a fog right now, don't panic. Don't freeze. Just trust the One who sees what you can't. He's not asking you to be flawless, just faithful.

**Prayer:**

Lord, I confess I like to know the plan, every step, every outcome. But Your Word reminds me to trust, not to take over. Help me lead through the fog with humility and courage. Give me the strength to move forward when all I have is faith in You. Amen.

# Day 14: The Long March

*"Let us not become weary in doing good, for at the proper time we will reap a harvest if we do not give up." - Galatians 6:9*

**Endurance Isn't Glamorous, But It's Holy**

There's a unique pain in the long march, when you've been walking for miles, gear digging into your back, legs burning, lips dry. You can't see the destination. The only thing that keeps you moving is the rhythm of the step in front of you. And the guy beside you.

Endurance doesn't get headlines. Nobody celebrates mile twenty when the finish line is still out of sight. But endurance is where battles are won, not in the flash of the first step, but in the faithfulness to keep stepping.

Ministry, parenting, marriage, recovery, missions, they all require the same thing: staying in the fight when everything in you wants to quit.

There have been seasons when I've begged God for a shortcut. When I've questioned whether the work mattered. When I felt unseen, unfruitful, and forgotten. But in those moments, this truth anchored me: *we will reap a harvest, if we don't give up.*

The fruit may take longer than you hoped. The victory may come after you feel spent. But if you're doing good, pouring into people, sowing seeds in faith, it *will* produce something eternal.

So don't stop. Not today. Not now.

Even if it feels like a slow march through mud, every step counts. And someone else might just find the strength to keep going because they saw you refuse to quit.

**Prayer:**

God, strengthen me for the long road. When I grow weary, renew my vision. When I feel discouraged, remind me that You see every act of obedience, even the ones no one else does. Help me press on with purpose and trust that You will bring the harvest. Amen.

# Day 15: The Weight of Command

*"Obey your leaders and submit to them, for they are keeping watch over your souls, as those who will have to give an account." -Hebrews 13:17a*

## Leadership Is a Burden Meant to Be Carried with Fear and Trembling

Command isn't about power, it's about responsibility. I learned that the hard way. As a squad leader, when one of my soldiers made a mistake, it didn't just reflect on them, it reflected on *me*. If someone didn't come home, I carried that weight. Authority wasn't a badge; it was a burden. And that burden didn't end when I left the military. In many ways, it only grew heavier.

Now I lead as a husband, father, nonprofit director, and follower of Christ. And there are days I still feel the pressure of every decision, every late-night prayer, every moment where someone is counting on me to show up, even when I'm running on fumes.

This verse in Hebrews reminds me: leadership isn't about being in control. It's about *keeping watch over souls*. That's heavy. And sacred. And not something to take lightly.

It also means I'm accountable, not just to people, but to God.

But here's the hope: we're not meant to carry the weight alone. When you submit your leadership to Jesus, you don't just bear the burden, you share it. He gives wisdom when you ask. He gives strength when you admit weakness. He gives grace for every imperfect but faithful "yes."

If you're in a position of leadership, whether over many or just one, don't shrug it off. And don't carry it alone. This calling is holy. And it's worth it.

**Prayer:**

Lord, thank You for entrusting me with influence, however big or small it may be. Help me to lead not with pride, but with humility, reverence, and love. Remind me that I lead under Your authority and for Your glory. Give me strength to carry the weight, and wisdom to lay it at Your feet. Amen.

# Day 16: No One Left Behind

*"My brothers, if one of you should wander from the truth and someone should bring him back, remember this: whoever turns a sinner from the error of his way will save him from death and cover over a multitude of sins." –*
*James 5:19–20*

**Pursue the One Who's Slipping Away**

In combat, if a soldier goes missing, the mission changes. Everything stops until they're found. It doesn't matter how dangerous or inconvenient it is, we go after them. Because we don't leave anyone behind. Period.

That same principle should guide us as spiritual leaders, as brothers, sisters, pastors, parents, mentors. But too often, when someone slips, morally, spiritually, emotionally, we let them go. Maybe out of awkwardness. Maybe out of fear. Maybe because we're tired or don't know what to say.

But James makes it clear: *if someone wanders, and you bring them back.  you're literally saving a life.*

I've had to be that guy. I've sat across from men who were ready to walk away from their family, their faith, or even their life. And I've been the one who needed someone to come after me too.

Restoration isn't about perfection. It's about pursuit. Jesus left the 99 to go after the one. That's not just a beautiful idea, it's a strategy. It's a lifestyle.

There is someone in your life right now who's slipping. Drifting. Fading from the fold. Don't ignore the tug. Don't wait until it's too late. Reach out. Speak truth. Sit in the mess with them. Call them back, gently, prayerfully, persistently. That's what shepherds do. And it's what soldiers do, too.

**Prayer:**

Jesus, give me Your heart for the one who is wandering. Give me courage to speak truth in love, and patience to walk with people through the valley. Make me bold enough to pursue those who are slipping, not in judgment, but in mercy. Help me love like You do. Amen.

# Day 17: The War Inside

*"So, I find this law at work: Although I want to do good, evil is right there with me... What a wretched man I am! Who will rescue me from this body of death? Thanks be to God, through Jesus Christ our Lord!"- Romans 7:21, 24–25*

## The Greatest Battle You'll Fight Is the One Within

I've fought enemies overseas, watched IEDs tear through convoys, and lost brothers in arms. But the most relentless, exhausting fight I've ever faced hasn't been on a battlefield, it's been inside my own head and heart.

The war inside doesn't stop when the shooting does. The enemy changes tactics. He whispers lies, dredges up shame, tempts you with shortcuts, and exhausts you with guilt. I've wrestled with anger I didn't understand, temptations I thought I'd conquered, and regrets that echoed in the silence long after the noise faded.

Paul got it. He didn't sugarcoat it. Even as an apostle, he said, *"What a wretched man I am!"* Not because he didn't love Jesus, but because he realized how fierce the battle for holiness really is. But he didn't stay stuck in shame, he lifted his eyes. *"Thanks be to God, through Jesus Christ our Lord!"*

Victory in the war within doesn't come by willpower or performance. It comes by surrender. By admitting we can't win on our own. By inviting Jesus to lead the charge inside us.

If you're tired of the internal fight, you're not broken, you're human. And you're not alone. But you *do* have a choice: to fight alone... or to hand the battle over to the One who's already won it.

**Prayer:**

Lord, You see the battles I hide. The thoughts, the struggles, the shame. I don't want to fight alone anymore. I surrender the war inside to You. Be my victory. Lead me in truth. And remind me daily that I am not condemned, I am redeemed. Amen.

# Day 18: Hold the Line

*"Be on your guard; stand firm in the faith; be courageous; be strong. Do everything in love."* - 1 Corinthians 16:13–14

## Stand Your Ground, But Don't Forget Why You're Standing

There are moments in combat when retreat isn't an option. The order comes down: *Hold the line.* No matter how outnumbered, how tired, how uncertain you feel, you dig in and stand firm. Because what's behind you is worth protecting.

That's how we're called to live as believers. Culture shifts. Temptation rises. Accusations come. And sometimes, the people you thought would stand with you fall away. It's in those moments that this verse hits like a call to arms: *Be on guard. Stand firm. Be courageous. Be strong. Do everything in love.*

That last part matters. *Do everything in love.*

It's easy to stand firm and become hard-hearted. To protect truth but forget grace. To defend conviction but lose compassion. But real strength, Christlike strength, looks like both courage *and* kindness. Resolve *and* gentleness. Grit *and* grace.

I've seen what happens when people only fight. And I've seen what happens when people only love but forget to stand. The enemy wins both ways. But when we hold the line with love, rooted in truth, anchored in Christ, we become the kind of leaders the world can follow.

Whatever line you're holding, in your home, in your faith, in your calling, don't let go. But don't harden either. Stand strong. And stay tender.

**Prayer:**

Jesus, help me to hold the line in the places You've called me to stand. Give me strength without pride, conviction without cruelty, and love that doesn't waver. Let me be known not just for what I stand *against*, but for how I stand *for* You, and for others. Amen.

# Day 19: The Debrief

*"Search me, God, and know my heart; test me and know my anxious thoughts. See if there is any offensive way in me, and lead me in the way everlasting." - Psalm 139:23–24*

**Reflection Is Where Growth Begins**

Every mission ends with a debrief. We gather around, sometimes exhausted, sometimes emotional, sometimes silent, and we talk it through. What went right? What failed? What did we miss? It's not just about blame, it's about learning. We don't grow without review.

I've learned to build spiritual debriefs into my life too. Especially after hard seasons, the ones where I feel spiritually bruised, emotionally drained, or battle worn. I've had to ask myself the hard questions: *Where did I let fear win? Where did pride sneak in? Did I lead with humility, or just with results?*

And when I've dared to ask, God has been faithful to answer. Not with shame, but with clarity.

Not to crush me, but to *refine* me.

Psalm 139 is David's version of a spiritual debrief: *Search me. Know me. Test me. Lead me.* That's the heart of a mature soldier, not just charging into battle, but submitting to correction, growth, and direction.

If you've just come through a storm, a mission, or a mistake, don't skip the debrief. Invite God into the mess. Let Him show you what needs to change, not so He can punish you, but so He can *lead* you toward what's next.

You won't grow from what you don't examine. And the mission ahead will demand a better version of you than the one who just came through the last fight.

**Prayer:**

Father, search my heart. Show me what I can't see. Reveal the blind spots, the habits, the wounds, and the pride that need to be addressed. Thank You that Your correction is love, not condemnation. Lead me forward with fresh clarity and deeper trust. Amen.

# Day 20: Carrying the Colors

*"Whatever you do, work at it with all your heart, as working for the Lord, not for human masters."*
*- Colossians 3:23*

**You Represent More Than Yourself**

In the military, carrying the colors, the flag, is an honor. The one who bears them doesn't just walk into a room; they represent every name, every sacrifice, every value stitched into the fabric of that banner. It's not about them, it's about what they stand for.

As believers, we carry something even greater. Wherever we go, into meetings, mission fields, hospital rooms, school drop-offs, or late-night conversations, we bear the name of Christ. People watch how we live, how we speak, how we love, how we respond when things fall apart. And they make judgments not just about *us*... but about the One we represent.

That used to weigh heavy on me. I didn't want to mess up the message. But over time, I've learned that carrying the colors of Christ isn't about performing with perfection, it's about serving with authenticity. It's about showing up with integrity. Owning your failures. Loving without conditions. Working with excellence, not for applause, but because it honors the One who sent you.

Whether you're in a uniform or a T-shirt, behind a pulpit or pushing a grocery cart, your life preaches something. Make sure it's pointing to the right Kingdom.

**Prayer:**

Jesus, help me carry Your name with honor today. Not in pride, but in humility. Not for recognition, but for reflection, that others might see You in me. Give me a heart to serve with excellence, speak with grace, and live with integrity. Let my life tell the truth about who You are. Amen.

# Day 21: Mission Creep

*"But seek first the kingdom of God and his righteousness, and all these things will be given to you as well." - Matthew 6:33*

**Stay Focused on What Matters Most**

In combat operations, there's a term we dreaded: *mission creep.* It happens when the original objective gets buried under added tasks, shifting priorities, or outside pressures. Before long, you're spread too thin, exposed, and far from what you were sent to do. It's not just a battlefield problem, it's a spiritual one, too.

I've experienced it firsthand. I've been called to serve or lead in a clear direction, only to find myself slowly drifting, not because I was rebellious, but because I got *busy.* Good things started crowding out the *best* things. Suddenly I was exhausted, scattered, reactive instead of obedient.

Jesus made it simple: *Seek first the Kingdom.* That's not just a nice verse; it's a course correction. When I recalibrate around that, everything else starts to fall into place, not perfectly, but purposefully. My work finds meaning again. My schedule makes more sense. My family gets my best instead of my leftovers. The fog starts to lift.

Mission creep is sneaky. It doesn't shout, it whispers. That's why we need daily realignment. Daily surrender. Daily reminders of the mission we've *really* been given love God, love people, make disciples.

Don't let your calling get buried in distractions. Lock in. Refocus. And move with purpose.

**Prayer:**

God, help me recognize when I've drifted. Show me where I've allowed distractions to take priority over obedience. Bring me back to the center, to seek Your Kingdom first. Refine my focus, restore my fire, and help me live every day on-mission for You. Amen.

# Day 22: The Cost of the Call

*"Then he said to them all: 'Whoever wants to be my disciple must deny themselves and take up their cross daily and follow me.'" - Luke 9:23*

## Calling Comes with a Price Tag, But It's Worth It

Before any mission, there's a briefing. We talk through objectives, risks, resources, timelines, and we count the cost. Not just in gear or logistics, but in lives. Every leader knows: you don't step into a mission lightly.

Jesus gave His own version of a mission briefing when He said, *"If you want to follow Me, it's going to cost you."* Deny yourself. Carry a cross. Follow, daily. This isn't casual Christianity.

It's a calling to die to yourself so that others might live. When I signed up to serve my country, I knew there would be a cost. But when I said yes to following Christ, I don't think I fully grasped it. I didn't realize it would mean forgiving people who hurt me, sacrificing comfort, missing time with family, facing loneliness, pushing a wheelchair through places most people avoid, and staying faithful when nobody sees.

But I also didn't realize the *joy* that would come. The peace. The purpose. The tears in a house parent's eyes when they hear, "You're not forgotten." The kid who feels hope for the first time. The moment someone says, "I met Jesus because you didn't quit."

Yes, the call is costly. But the Kingdom return is eternal.

Don't be afraid of the cost. Just make sure what you're spending your life on is worth it. Because you're going to spend it either way.

**Prayer:**

Jesus, I want to follow You, not just when it's easy, but when it costs something. Help me deny myself daily and take up the cross You've called me to carry. Give me joy in sacrifice, courage in surrender, and a heart fully committed to the mission You've given me. Amen.

# Day 23: Sacred Ground

*"Do not come any closer," God said. "Take off your sandals, for the place where you are standing is holy ground." - Exodus 3:5*

## God Often Shows Up in the Unlikeliest Places

We tend to think of holy ground as a place, a church, a sanctuary, a peaceful mountaintop. But in my life, some of the holiest moments have happened in places that didn't feel holy at all.

I've met God in hospital rooms, beside broken beds in orphanages, in muddy fields in Eastern Europe, and during late-night breakdowns when I had nothing left to offer. I've felt His presence more in tears than in triumph. More in broken prayers than polished sermons.

Moses encountered God in the middle of a desert, not in a temple, but by a bush that caught fire and didn't burn out. What made that ground holy wasn't the location, it was the presence of the Lord.

The same is true for you. Your wheelchair can become sacred ground. Your kitchen table. Your office. Your foxhole. Your late-night drive. Wherever God meets you, that's holy. Wherever you stop and listen, that's sacred.

So, stop waiting for a perfect setting. Stop believing the lie that God only moves in big events or clean places. He meets us in the mess. And sometimes the holiest thing you can do is take off your shoes, slow down, strip off pride, and recognize that He's already here.

**Prayer:**

Lord, open my eyes to see that You're present even here, even now. Help me to recognize the sacred in the ordinary, the holy in the hard places. Teach me to pause, to listen, and to worship on whatever ground You place beneath my feet. I want to meet You today, wherever I am. Amen.

# Day 24: The Ministry of Presence

*"Rejoice with those who rejoice; mourn with those who mourn." - Romans 12:15*

## Sometimes the Strongest Thing You Can Do Is Show Up

There's a moment every soldier knows, when a teammate's down, and there's nothing to say. You just kneel beside them. You bleed with them. You carry them if you can. You *don't leave*.

That's presence. And sometimes, it's more powerful than any words you could offer. I used to think ministry had to be polished, sermons, strategy, leadership. But then I found myself holding the hands of kids in Moldova who had lost everything. Or sitting next to a mom in Ukraine who didn't need a speech, she needed someone to sit in the ashes with her.

The most healing moments I've witnessed didn't come from a pulpit. They came from proximity. From being present. From showing up when it was uncomfortable or inconvenient. From *mourning with those who mourn*, not fixing, just being.

You don't need the perfect words. You don't need a title. You need a heart that's willing to be interrupted. Feet willing to go. Arms willing to hold. Ears willing to listen.

In a world full of noise, presence is a rare and sacred gift. Jesus embodied this. He didn't just shout truth from heaven; He stepped into our pain. He came close. He stayed close.

Let's do the same.

**Prayer:**

Jesus, thank You for not staying distant. You came close. You wept with the broken. You sat with the outcast. Teach me to do the same. Help me resist the urge to fix and instead learn to simply *be there*. Use my presence to reflect Yours. Amen.

# Day 25: When the Mission Changes

*"Many are the plans in a person's heart, but it is the Lord's purpose that prevails." –*
*Proverbs 19:21*

**Flexibility Is Faith in Action**

Every soldier learns this truth early: no plan survives first contact. You train, you prep, you rehearse, but the moment the real-world hits, things change. And when they do, your job isn't to complain. It's to adapt. Improvise. Adjust.

I had plans for my life. Career goals. Physical strength. A "normal" future. But after the blast, everything shifted. I walked off the battlefield, but I didn't walk back into the life I had imagined. Over time, the injuries caught up with me, and I eventually found myself in a wheelchair, entering a life I never expected. At first, I saw it as a detour. Now I see it as divine redirection.

The mission didn't end. It changed.

And maybe that's where you are today, staring at a new diagnosis, a closed door, a canceled dream, or a calling you never asked for. It's okay to grieve it. But don't confuse a change in orders with the end of your purpose.

God's mission hasn't stopped. It's moving forward, through you, even here. The men and women I serve alongside, especially those who've lost limbs, careers, or loved ones, are proof that you don't need ideal circumstances to have eternal impact. You just need a heart that says, *"Yes, Lord. Even now."*

Be flexible. Be faithful. The battlefield may have shifted, but the war is still worth fighting.

**Prayer:**

Lord, I trust You even when the path changes. Help me surrender my plans and embrace Your purpose. Teach me to adapt with faith instead of fear. Remind me that no matter where I find myself, You still have a mission for me. I'm reporting for duty, again. Amen.

# Day 26: Light in the Trenches

*"The light shines in the darkness, and the darkness has not overcome it." - John 1:5*

## Hope Doesn't Have to Shout, It Just Has to Shine

I've spent nights in the trenches, literal ones and spiritual ones. I've seen the kind of darkness that makes you wonder if light will ever return. War zones. Psych wards. Quiet hotel rooms where the weight of it all comes crashing down. And yet, in every one of those places, I've seen something that darkness couldn't snuff out.

A flicker. A breath. A single, stubborn light.

Sometimes it came through a text from a friend at just the right time. Sometimes through a child's laughter. Sometimes it came through a verse that I'd thought I'd forgotten or a worship song I softly hummed when I didn't know what else to do. But it always came.

Because that's who Jesus is. He *is* the Light. Not just when things are clean and hopeful, but right there in the grime of the trenches.

You don't have to be the sun. You don't have to light up the whole sky. Sometimes, your job is to hold up one small flame of hope, and trust that it will be enough to push back the dark.

If you're in a trench right now, hold on. Light is coming. And if you're out of it, then be the one who brings the light to someone else. Even the smallest flame changes the battlefield.

**Prayer:**

Jesus, shine in my darkness. Remind me that no trench is too deep for Your presence. When I feel like I have nothing left to give, help me hold up just one light of hope. And if someone near me is struggling, give me the courage to step into their darkness with love and truth. Amen.

# Day 27: The Honor of Obedience

*"If you love me, keep my commands." – John 14:15*

**Obedience Is More Than Duty, It's Devotion**

In the military, obedience isn't optional, it's how people stay alive. But the best soldiers don't follow orders just out of fear. They obey out of respect. Loyalty. Honor. They trust the one giving the command.

That's the kind of obedience Jesus wants from us, not robotic, fearful compliance, but love-driven surrender.

There have been times in my life when obedience cost me deeply. Leaving opportunities. Telling hard truths. Walking into uncomfortable rooms. Forgiving when I didn't feel like it. Saying "yes" when everything in me wanted to say, "not now." But every time I obeyed, even when it was hard, I found a deeper intimacy with God on the other side.

Obedience is where relationship becomes real. It's one thing to *believe* in Jesus. It's another thing to *follow* Him when it's inconvenient, unpopular, or unclear.

Sometimes obedience means staying. Sometimes it means going. Sometimes it means sacrificing your comfort for someone else's healing. But it always means trusting that the One who gave the command is good, and that His plans are better than ours.

If you've been wrestling with something God is asking of you, take a step. It may feel small, but obedience always echoes. And on the other side, you'll find the smile of your Commander.

**Prayer:**

Lord, help me to obey not out of obligation, but out of love. Give me ears to hear Your voice, and courage to follow wherever You lead. When obedience costs me, remind me that You are worth every sacrifice. Make me faithful in the small things, and bold in the big ones. Amen.

# Day 28: Strength for the Stretch

*"But those who hope in the Lord will renew their strength. They will soar on wings like eagles; they will run and not grow weary; they will walk and not be faint." - Isaiah 40:31*

**God Doesn't Just Call You, He Sustains You**

The hardest part of any mission isn't always the beginning or the battle; it's the stretch in between. The long, slow, steady march when the adrenaline is gone, the goal still seems far away, and your body aches to stop. That's where endurance is tested. That's where faith is forged.

I've lived in that stretch. As a disabled vet, as a husband rebuilding trust, as a leader in ministry facing spiritual fatigue, I've felt the weight of "not yet." I've known what it's like to run on empty, to smile through the ache, to serve when no one sees. And I've learned something priceless in the process: God doesn't just call you, He *carries* you.

Isaiah 40 doesn't say the strong will make it. It says those who *hope in the Lord* will renew their strength. That means the strength isn't manufactured, it's received. It's given fresh, not earned through the grind. And sometimes, God won't remove the stretch, because He's using it to stretch *you*.

Wherever you are today, soaring, running, or barely walking, know this: He sees you. He hasn't forgotten you. And His strength is still present, still sufficient, and still renewing you for this stretch of the journey. Don't give up now. Your second wind is coming.

**Prayer:**

God, I need Your strength. Not just for the fight, but for the stretch, the slow middle where faith can grow cold. Renew me today. Help me to wait on You with expectancy, not anxiety. Carry me when I can't carry myself. And remind me that You are enough for every step. Amen.

# Day 29: Victory Looks Different Here

*"But thanks be to God! He gives us the victory through our Lord Jesus Christ."*
*- 1 Corinthians 15:57*

## The Win Isn't Always What You Think

In the military, victory usually means taking ground, completing the mission, bringing your people home. It's marked by flags raised, enemies defeated, objectives met. Clean wins. Clear results.

But after I came home, in a wheelchair, battling TBI and PTSD, trying to lead a new kind of life, I had to redefine victory. I had to learn that sometimes victory isn't walking across a finish line.

Sometimes it's *crawling* across with your soul intact. Sometimes it's not quitting on your family. Sometimes it's choosing joy when you could choose bitterness. Sometimes it's praying one more time when everything feels silent.

Victory in the Kingdom looks different. It's not about appearances. It's about faithfulness. It's not about never falling; it's about always getting back up. And ultimately, it's not about what *you* can do... but what *Christ* already did.

The cross looked like a defeat. The tomb looked like the end. But those were just the battlefields God used to show us what victory *really* means: sin conquered. Death undone. Grace poured out. Hope secured.

So whatever battle you're in, whether it feels like you're winning or losing, remember this: if you're in Christ, the outcome has already been decided. You don't fight *for* victory. You fight *from* it.

**Prayer:**

Jesus, thank You that I don't have to earn the win, You already secured it. Help me see victory through Your eyes, not the world's. Teach me to celebrate faithfulness over flash, obedience over outcomes. And when I'm weary, remind me: I am already more than a conqueror in You. Amen.

# Day 30: Still Standing

*"Now to him who is able to keep you from stumbling and to present you before his glorious presence without fault and with great joy, to the only God our Savior be glory, majesty, power and authority, through Jesus Christ our Lord..." - Jude 1:24–25*

## You're Not Just Surviving, You're Still Serving

Some days I look at my life, the wheelchair, the scars, the missed moments, the people we've buried, and I marvel that I'm still here. Not just breathing. Still *serving*. Still *leading*. Still *standing*, even if it doesn't always look like it used to.

I used to think "standing" meant strength, upright, unshaken, moving fast. But now I know that standing can look like showing up. Like praying again. Like pushing forward inch by inch. Like refusing to let your past define your purpose.

I've stood in fire. I've stood in failure. I've stood in places I never imagined God would send me, orphanages, Capitol offices, campgrounds, and hospital rooms. And every place has reminded me of one thing: He's the One holding me up. I am still standing, *not because of me*, but because of Him. And so are you.

If you're reading this, you've made it through 30 days of leaning in, pressing on, and letting God reshape your view of what it means to be both a soldier and a shepherd. You've been called. You've been tested. And now, you're being sent, again.

Keep showing up. Keep loving deeply. Keep enduring hardship like a good soldier. Keep leading like a gentle shepherd. And above all, never forget Who's holding you up.

**Prayer:**

Father, thank You for sustaining me, for carrying me through wounds, weariness, and warfare. I give You all the glory for the ground I've covered and all the hope for the ground still ahead. Keep me faithful. Keep me humble. And keep me standing in Your strength until the mission is complete. Amen.

# A Soldier's Charge, A Shepherd's Blessing

You made it through these 30 days, but this isn't the finish line. It's a handoff.

A soldier doesn't train to feel motivated. He trains to be faithful when motivation is gone. And a shepherd doesn't care for sheep when it's convenient, he stays when it's costly. That's the kind of life Jesus calls us into steady obedience, quiet courage, and love that shows up.

So, here's my charge to you:

- Stay close to the Shepherd. Don't drift. Don't numb. Don't isolate.

- Keep your heart soft and your standards high.

- Lead someone. Serve someone. Forgive someone.

- Do the next right thing, especially when it's hard.

- And when you fall, don't quit. Get back up, repent quickly, and keep walking.

**Prayer:**

Lord Jesus, make me steady. Make me humble. Make me brave. Teach my hands to serve and my heart to listen. Give me the courage to obey You in the hidden places and the strength to love people when it costs me something. Keep me close to You, the Shepherd of my soul, and let my life point others home. Amen.

# Group & Personal Reflection Guide

Use these with any day in the devotional:

1. What phrase, image, or sentence stood out most and why?

2. What does this day reveal about God's character?

3. What does it reveal about my heart right now?

4. Where am I tempted to drift: faith, family, integrity, purity, purpose, or peace?

5. What's one area where I need to repent quickly and reset?

6. What's one "next right thing" I can do in the next 24 hours?

7. Who is God asking me to serve, encourage, or lead this week?

8. What would obedience look like if I removed fear and pride from the equation?
9. What resistance do I feel, and what might that resistance be protecting?
10. What's one prayer I'm willing to pray with full honesty today?

Optional group closer: "One takeaway + one action + one prayer request."

# Scripture Index

Day 21 — Matthew 6:33

Day 22 — Luke 9:23

Day 23 — Exodus 3:5

Day 24 — Romans 12:15

Day 25 — Proverbs 19:21

Day 26 — John 1:5

Day 27 — John 14:15

Day 28 — Isaiah 40:31

Day 29 — 1 Corinthians 15:57

Day 30 — Jude 1:24–25

# Topic Index

# Keep Walking

You finished 30 days, now let it become a way of life.

If you don't know what to do next, keep it simple and stay faithful:

**A daily rhythm:**

1. Read one passage of Scripture
2. Pray one honest prayer
3. Do one act of obedience
4. Encourage one person

**A weekly rhythm:**

- Meet with your fire team (or build one)
- Debrief with God (Psalm 139:23–24)
- Serve someone who can't repay you

If you want to run this devotional again, don't read it faster, read it deeper. Carry one verse for a full week and live it out.

## Author Bio

JD Drinkard is a retired U.S. Army Sergeant First Class, combat veteran, and founder of the Mighty Warrior Foundation and International Leadership Solutions. After surviving an IED blast that led to a traumatic brain injury and years of invisible wounds, JD found a deeper calling, to serve not just as a soldier, but as a shepherd.

Now an adaptive athlete, nonprofit leader, and ministry partner in Eastern Europe, JD speaks hope into broken places. Whether mentoring fatherless boys in Moldova, advocating for wounded veterans, or leading discipleship programs for churches, his mission is simple: live faithfully, lead humbly, and never leave a soul behind.

*A Soldier's Heart, A Shepherd's Calling* was born from the battlefield and refined through service. JD writes with honesty, grit, and Gospel-centered conviction, reminding others that even in weakness, we are still called to lead.

JD also serves through missions with Roads of Hope, sits on the board of Healing4Heroes, and is a founder and committee member for IGY6–Gulf Coast. He champions inclusivity and celebrates overcoming disability through his involvement in the U.S. Wheelchair Football League (USWFL), Move United Warfighters, Wounded Warrior Project, Veterans of Foreign Wars (VFW) and Disabled American Veterans (DAV). He is currently pursuing his MBA at the University of Alabama.

JD lives by the words of 2 Timothy 2:3 - "Endure hardship with us like a good soldier of Christ Jesus."

Connect: www.jddrinkard.com | jd@ilsconsulting.org